Synchro Swans

Written by Sandy Roydhouse
Photography by Dan Helms

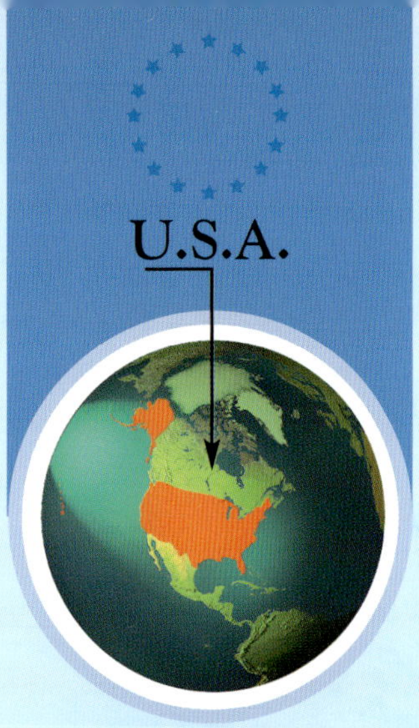

Divali Ramkalawan lives in Los Angeles, California. Being part of a team such as the Synchro Swans takes a great deal of **commitment**. Divali has to carefully manage her time so that she can fit everything into one day—swim practice, school, homework, and relaxing with her friends.

commitment being involved wholeheartedly

Contents

Synchro Swans 4

Explore the U.S.A. 14

New York City 16

Opening Up the West 18

Movie Town 20

The Aloha State 22

What Do You Think? 24

Index 24

Synchro Swans

Most people are still sleeping at sunrise, but this is when the Synchro Swans are hard at work!

The Synchro Swans is a synchronized swimming team from Los Angeles, California. Synchronized swimming is a sport in which members of a team perform dance-like movements in a swimming pool. They match their movements, both under the water and above, to each other and to music. The sport is a combination of swimming, dancing, and gymnastics.

synchronize to arrange events so that they happen at the same time

Besides hard work, what other qualities would you need to be part of a team such as the Synchro Swans?

In addition to swimming, Divali Ramkalawan loves dancing and gymnastics, so synchronized swimming is the perfect sport for her. While she often finds it difficult to fit everything into her day, Divali knows that the hard work she and her teammates put into their practice sessions makes the team stand out from its competition.

During the summer, the Synchro Swans train in the early morning three times a week. The girls are dedicated to their sport and, with the help of their coaches, perform routines that are full of imagination and energy. They are eager to compete against other teams, because they want to reach the top of their sport in the United States. They are already well on their way. They have more creative dance movements than many of the teams they compete against.

dedicate to give time and effort to something

The Synchro Swans started in 1998 with only three members. In just two years, the number of members increased to twenty-five. Today, both senior and junior teams compete at the state level. All the girls dream of one day competing at the Olympic Games.

Olympic Dreams

Originally known as water ballet, the term *synchronized swimming* was first used in Canada in the 1920s. It spread to the United States in the 1930s.

Synchronized swimming became a competitive sport in 1941, and in 1984, it became an Olympic sport. U.S. synchronized swimming teams have won at least one medal at each of the Olympic events since. At the 2004 Olympic Games in Athens, Greece, the U.S. synchronized swimming team (above) won a bronze medal.

The Synchro Swans know that "practice makes perfect." Most of their practice sessions take place underwater. The coach uses an underwater speaker to pump music to the girls. She also hooks up a microphone to the underwater speaker. Then she can talk to the girls even when they're upside down, underwater!

Like dancers, it's important for synchro swimmers to keep in time. Their legs and arms must move at exactly the same time. When they surface, they must break the water simultaneously. Each movement must be practiced over and over again.

The underwater speaker allows Divali to take instructions from her coach.

simultaneous happening at the same time

Did You Know?

- Synchro swimmers must not touch the bottom of the pool at any time during a routine.
- Synchro swimmers keep their eyes open underwater. This helps them stay in time with their teammates.
- The most important piece of equipment for synchro swimmers is a nose plug. It keeps water out of their nose, even when they are upside down!
- Swimmers are sometimes underwater for up to one minute!
- A synchro routine starts with deckwork. This sets the mood but doesn't count for any points.

On land, the girls practice the same drills that they practice underwater. These drills make up different parts of their routine. Synchronized swimming involves finely tuned movements, great strength, and flexibility. There's a lot for the girls to remember. They need to memorize the basic movements so that they don't have to think when they're performing. This allows them to concentrate on their new movements, their breathing, and staying in time with each other. Sometimes, all their effort goes toward staying underwater. This can be very difficult if the girls are tired or running out of breath!

flexible able to bend easily

Sculling is an arm movement a little like paddling. The girls practice sculling to help them keep their heads underwater and their legs straight.

The coaches of both senior and junior teams know their girls are capable of achieving even quicker, more difficult movements. They are preparing the girls for tougher competition.

Moving in a circle, half submerged and in time with the other girls, takes a great deal of concentration by the members of the junior team.

Members of the 2004 U.S. synchronized swimming team are great role models for the Synchro Swans. Hard work and dedication to the sport paid off for this team when they won a bronze medal at the 2004 Olympic Games in Athens, Greece.

Explore the U.S.A.

The United States of America has the third largest population in the world and is the fourth largest country in area. It stretches from the Pacific Ocean in the west to the Atlantic Ocean in the east. It is made up of fifty states, and each state has its own state capital and governor.

Washington, D.C., is the capital of the United States. It has many beautiful buildings, statues, and memorials. Washington, D.C., is home to diplomats from all over the world. The President of the United States lives in the White House. The Congress of the United States, which makes the laws for the nation, meets at the Capitol Building in Washington, D.C.

The White House (left) has been well preserved by the presidents who have lived there. It looks almost exactly as it did when it was first occupied in 1800.

diplomat a person who represents his or her government in another country

Building first began on the Capitol in Washington, D.C., in 1793. The original building was completed in 1826; however, Congress has been meeting there since 1800. Today, the building is also used for important national ceremonies such as swearing in a new president.

On the Go!

About how many people live in the largest city in the U.S.?

Go to page 16

What is the Oregon Trail?

Go to page 18

Which city in the U.S. has a royal palace?

Go to page 22

New York City

The United States is famous for its cities. Skyscrapers were first built in the U.S., and today almost every city has a skyline filled with tall buildings. New York City, on the east coast, is the largest city in the United States. Just over eight million people live there. This is more than twice the number of people in the second largest city, Los Angeles.

The Empire State Building, the Statue of Liberty, and Times Square are attractions that bring thousands of tourists to New York each year.

The United States has been called "a nation of immigrants," because millions of people from all around the world have moved there to live. Hundreds of different languages are spoken throughout the U.S.

The harbor in New York City is one of the busiest harbors in the United States. Because it is a deep-water harbor, it can handle large ships and is one of the major centers for international trade.

Thanksgiving

In 1620 a group called the pilgrims sailed from England on the *Mayflower* in search of a new home where they could practice their religion. They arrived in what is now Plymouth, Massachusetts, and founded one of the first European settlements.

The first Thanksgiving feast was held in 1621. Among the guests at that first Thanksgiving were ninety-one Native Americans who helped the pilgrims survive their first difficult year. On the fourth Thursday in November, Americans continue the tradition with a Thanksgiving dinner for family and friends.

Opening Up the West

Gold! In the 1840s, people from all around the world rushed to California in search of gold. The population of California soared, and business boomed. Many people in the gold-mining business made fortunes. So, too, did the store owners who supplied the miners with food, tools, and clothing.

After the gold rush, many pioneers stayed on in California and developed agricultural industries, such as fruit farming. News spread quickly about the unsettled land and the mild climate. From the 1840s to the 1860s, thousands more people moved west. One popular route they took west over the Rocky Mountains was known as the Oregon Trail.

These children are trying their luck "panning" for gold in a river in Denver, Colorado, much like gold prospectors did in the 1840s.

pioneer a person who explores an unknown area and settles there

Today, tourists can take a trip along the Oregon Trail in a horse-drawn, covered wagon. The trip gives them firsthand experience of the lives of pioneers in the 1800s seeking a new life in the west.

If you were traveling along the Oregon Trail for the first time, what problems might you expect to face along the way?

Descendants of Oregon Trail settlers meet at the stone that marks the trail's end.

Movie Town

Los Angeles on the west coast is the second largest city in the U.S. The mild climate allows people to enjoy outdoor activities all year round. Hollywood, which is part of Los Angeles, is the center of the movie industry. The huge Hollywood sign, a well-known landmark, was built into the hills above the district in 1922. Each letter is more than 45 feet tall!

Universal Studios in Hollywood is a popular tourist attraction where people can find out how movies are made, visit movie sets, and enjoy roller-coaster rides. Hollywood Boulevard has more than 2,000 bronze stars set in the sidewalk, each bearing the name of a different movie star or celebrity. Thousands of tourists visit this "Walk of Fame" every year.

Universal Studios

celebrity a famous person

HOLLYWOOD

The Aloha State

The islands of Hawaii became the 50th U.S. state in 1959. The capital, Honolulu, is the only U.S. city located in the Tropics, the only U.S. city with a royal palace (`Iolani Palace), and the only U.S. city with an equal blend of western, Asian, and Polynesian people.

Hawaii is a popular vacation destination for people from all around the world. They travel there to enjoy the beautiful beaches, warm tropical waters, boating, golf, and other pastimes. The state's main industries are tourism, agriculture—especially pineapples, sugar cane, and flowers—and fishing.

`Iolani Palace was the official home of King Kalakaua and his Queen, Kapi`olani, from 1882 until the king's death in 1891. It is now a national historic landmark and a popular tourist attraction.

Although situated on a beautiful beach, downtown Honolulu is like many other U.S. cities. It is packed with high-rise buildings, many of which face one of the world's most famous beaches, Waikiki.

Did You Know?

Almost everyone in Hawaii speaks English; however, there is also a distinctive Hawaiian language. Because of the way the words are constructed, the language sounds quite musical to those who have never heard it. Some Hawaiian language rules are

- The Hawaiian alphabet has 12 letters.

AEHIKLMNOPUW

- Every Hawaiian word and syllable ends with a vowel.
- Two consonants never occur without a vowel between them.
- The accent of most words falls on the second to last syllable.

Can you see how the rules apply to these words?

aloha = hello

mele = song

mahi-mahi = fish

pua = flower

What Do You Think?

1 Members of the Synchro Swans must be "in sync" with each other on a personal level just as they are in their sport. How does this help them with their goals?

2 Synchronized swimming combines the skills of swimming, dancing, and gymnastics. What other sports are a mix of different skills?

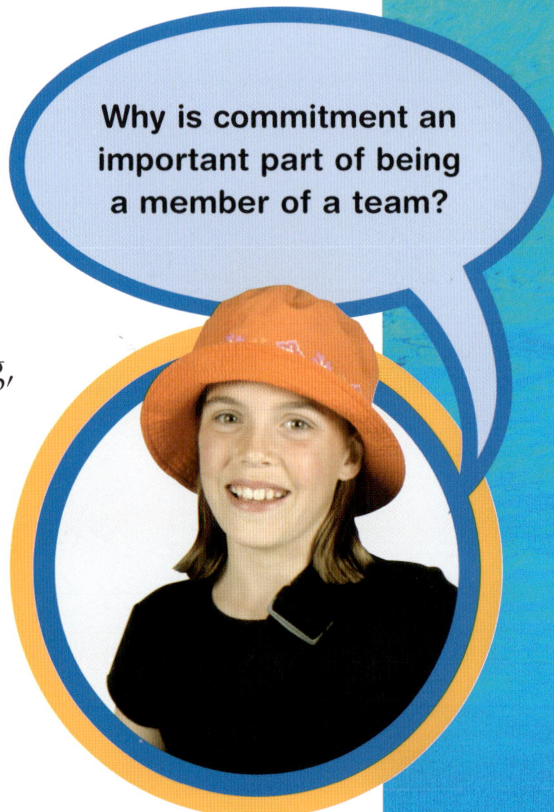

Index

Hawaii 22–23
Hollywood 15, 20–21
Los Angeles 4, 16, 20–21
New York 15–17
Olympic Games 7, 13
Oregon Trail 18–19
swimming 4–13
Thanksgiving 17
Universal Studios 20
Washington, D. C. 14–15